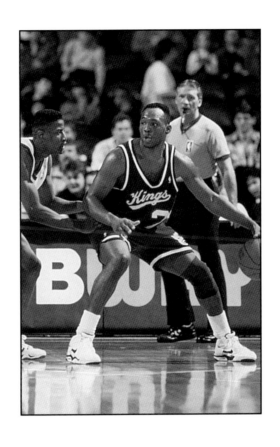

SACRAMENTO KINGS

MICHAEL E. GOODMAN

COVER AND TITLE PAGE PHOTOS BY MATT MAHURIN

CREATIVE EDUCATION

Published by Creative Education, Inc.

123 S. Broad Street, Mankato, Minnesota 56001 USA

Art Director, Rita Marshall
Cover and title page photography by Matt Mahurin
Book design by Rita Marshall

Photos by: Allsport; Mel Bailey; Bettmann Archive;
Brian Drake; Duomo; Focus On Sports; FPG; South
Florida Images Inc.; Spectra-Action; Sportschrome;
Sports Photo Masters, Inc.; SportsLight: Brian Drake,
Long Photography; Wide World Photos.

Library of Congress Cataloging-in-Publication Data

Goodman, Michael E.

Sacramento Kings / Michael E. Goodman.

Summary: Highlights the players, coaches, playing
strategies, and memorable games in the history of the
Sacramento Kings basketball team.

ISBN 0-88682-540-7

1. Sacramento Kings (Basketball team)—Juvenile
literature. [1. Sacramento Kings (Basketball team)—
History. 2. Basketball—History.] I. Title.

GV885.52.S24G66 1992   92-4538
796.323'64'0974811—dc20   CIP

SACRAMENTO: HOME OF THE KINGS

Sacramento, California, has always been a city with good luck. When it was founded in 1840, Sacramento was just a tiny settlement consisting of a small fort and a few log cabins. Then, eight years later, gold was discovered nearby at Sutter's Mill, and the California gold rush was on. Sacramento became a logical settling place for many of those wealth seekers, and by 1854 had grown enough in size and importance to be named the capital of California. A few years later, Sacramento also became the terminus of the Pony Express, which added to its stature. Today, a Pony Express Museum is one of the city's most popular tourist attractions, reminding locals and visitors alike of Sacramento's Old West beginnings.

The Kings were formerly known as the Royals.

In 1985, a new group of "settlers" arrived in Sacramento, hoping that some of the city's luck would rub off on them. They were members of the Sacramento Kings, a basketball team with a long history. The franchise was originally established in 1945 in Rochester, New York, and also settled for a time in Cincinnati, Ohio; Omaha, Nebraska; and Kansas City, Missouri. By the 1980s the Kings had fallen on hard times and were looking for a new home and new luck. They hoped to find both in Sacramento.

Bob Davies ran the Rochester offense and recorded a league-leading 321 assists in 60 games.

"Our city's good fortune continues," proclaimed Sacramento businessman Joe Benvenuti, one of the team's new owners, when he announced the Kings' move to Sacramento. Agreeing with Benvenuti, local residents quickly began pouring into tiny Sacramento Arena to watch their city's newest heroes. Unfortunately, the Sacramento Kings have not done as well in the standings of the National Basketball Association as they have done in the league attendance rankings. Their youth and enthusiasm, however, combined with their club's long tradition of winning and basketball excellence, should help them improve in the future.

A ROYAL START IN ROCHESTER

As befits their name, the Kings have regal roots. The club began its life in 1945 as the Rochester Royals in the old National Basketball League. Led by guards Al Cervi, Bob Davies, and Red Holzman, the Royals captured the NBL championship in their first year in the league. They stayed near the top of the NBL for two more seasons, and then moved to the Basketball Association of America in 1948. By the next season, the BAA and NBL had merged to form the NBA, and the Royals belonged to their third league.

The powerful Duane Causwell.

*During the Royals'
championship
season, Arnie Risen
led the team in
both scoring and
rebounding.*

The Royals might have gone down in history as the best team in the early years of pro basketball, had it not been for 6-foot-10 center George Mikan, the most dominant big man in the game in those days. Playing first for the Chicago Gears and then for the Minneapolis Lakers, Mikan led his teams to playoff victories over Rochester nearly every year in the late 1940s and early 1950s.

"When I started playing with Rochester, it was either us or Minneapolis that would win it all," said Royals star Bob Davies. "They had the big men and we had the good little men. That was the difference in a nutshell. It was murder playing against Mikan because when the Lakers needed two points, he'd get them. George Mikan cost me a lot of money in playoff bonuses and endorsements."

Rochester's luck against Minneapolis changed during the 1951 playoffs. This time, Mikan was out of action with a fractured foot, and the Royals edged the Lakers to reach the NBA finals against the New York Knicks.

Led by Davies, 6-foot guard Bob Wanzer, and 6-foot-9 center Arnie Risen, the heavily favored Royals routed the Knicks in the first three games of the best-of-seven series. Then the Knicks fought back with three straight victories of their own to set up a seventh-game showdown.

In game seven, the Royals roared out to a 13-3 lead, but the Knicks closed the gap to 40-34 by halftime. The contest was nip-and-tuck throughout the second half. With only 40 seconds left and the score tied 75-75, Bob Davies drove hard for a basket and crashed into Knicks guard Dick McGuire. The referee's whistle blew. Which way would the call go? "Blocking foul against McGuire," the ref shouted. Davies calmly sank both free throws, sealing the victory and the Royals' first (and only) NBA title.

THE BITTERSWEET STORY OF MAURICE STOKES

The Royals continued to make the playoffs over the next few years, but they could not quite maintain the quality and excitement of their championship season. The team's top players were aging, and the introduction of the 24-second clock to the NBA worked against the Royals' slow, ball-control offensive style. The Royals needed some new blood, and they found the youngsters they were seeking in the 1955 college draft—forward Jack Twyman and center Maurice Stokes. Both were gifted players, and they soon became inseparable friends. Their friendship is one of the most touching stories in sports history.

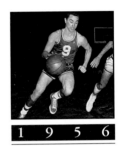

Bobby Wanzer played in every Royals game for the sixth straight year.

Stokes was an immediate hit in the NBA, while Twyman took a little longer to develop. In his rookie season, Stokes led the Royals in scoring, rebounding, assists, and minutes played, and led the entire league in rebounding. His all-around skills earned him the NBA Rookie of the Year award for 1956. Though he was only 6-foot-7, Stokes seemed much bigger on the court.

Stokes continued his fine play over the next two seasons and was named to the second-team All-NBA squad both years. Meanwhile, Twyman was also asserting himself as one of the league's top scorers and most accurate shooters. Yet these two gifted players could not turn around the fortunes of the Royals. The club finished dead last in the NBA in both 1955-56 and 1956-57. Fewer people began turning out for home games, which meant less revenue for the team's owners. Finally, before the 1957-58 season, the owners decided to move the franchise to a bigger city—Cincinnati, Ohio. The Royals had better luck there, tying for second place in the division and earning a berth in the playoffs.

Current star Mitch Richmond…

...reminds many fans of former great Nate Archibald.

For the third year in a row, Maurice Stokes recorded more than 1,000 points and 1,000 rebounds.

Unfortunately, the 1958 playoffs marked the end of the playing partnership of Maurice Stokes and Jack Twyman. During the last few weeks of the season, Stokes complained of headaches and blurred vision, but he decided to play in spite of those problems. In the offseason Stokes went to doctors, who discovered that the player was suffering from encephalitis, a disease sometimes known as "sleeping sickness." The illness began ravishing Stokes' nervous system, leaving him paralyzed and hospitalized. There was almost no hope for recovery.

The once-graceful athlete was now a helpless invalid. There was an additional problem to consider: Stokes' hospital and doctor bills had used up nearly all of his family's savings. How was he going to get the care he needed, and how was his family going to get along? That's when Jack Twyman stepped in. He began looking for ways to collect money to help Stokes. Also, to assist Stokes' family, Twyman had himself appointed his friend's legal guardian, which meant he would be responsible for Stokes' care. Twyman continued to serve as Stokes' guardian for nearly 13 years, until the stricken player's death in 1970. The Cincinnati forward appealed to his fellow players in the NBA to help out as well. At Twyman's request, many of the game's top stars turned out every year until Stokes' death for a special exhibition game held at a resort in upstate New York to raise money for the Maurice Stokes Fund.

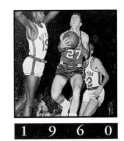

Jack Twyman became only the fourth man in league history to score 2,000 points in a season.

Jack Twyman was not only a great humanitarian, he was also a fine basketball player. By the early 1960s, Twyman had become a perennial NBA All-Star, averaging between 25 and 30 points per game. He was only the sixth player to score 15,000 points in a career, and went nearly eight seasons without missing a single game. Following his 11-year career with the Royals, Twyman was elected to the NBA Hall of Fame.

THE "BIG O" ARRIVES IN CINCI

Jack Twyman lost one talented teammate when Maurice Stokes became crippled, but he was soon to gain another skilled comrade. Following a three-year All-American career at the University of Cincinnati, Oscar Robertson joined the Royals before the 1960-61 season. He set the league on fire right away. During his rookie season, the "Big O" averaged more than 30 points, along with 10 rebounds and almost 10 assists per game. He then bettered all three marks the next season, becoming the first player ever to average a "triple-double"—double figures in three different statistical categories.

"Don't try to describe the man," said Jack Twyman of

Rookie Jerry Lucas set club records with 1,375 rebounds and a rebounding average of 17.4 per game.

his new teammate. "You can watch him, you can enjoy him, you can appreciate him, but you can't adequately describe him. It's not any one thing, it's his completeness that amazes you."

Soon it seemed that every player in the NBA had a classic "Big O" story to tell. "I remember we were playing the Royals one night, and somehow I ended up guarding Oscar after a switch," said San Francisco Warriors forward Tom Meschery. "Well, Oscar throws the ball behind his back, heads for the basket, and leaves me behind. It was a fantastic move, split-second like always with him. But just as the ball goes in, the referee calls traveling. Oscar got real excited and starts screaming at the ref, 'How can you call that traveling? You never saw that move before.'"

Robertson's confidence rubbed off on his Cincinnati teammates—players such as Twyman, center Wayne Embry, forward Bob Boozer, and guard Adrian Smith. By 1962-63, Robertson's third season with the club, the Royals had become a high-scoring squad that was a serious contender in the Eastern Division. That year, they took the powerful Boston Celtics all the way to a seventh game during the Division playoff finals. With a few more breaks, the Royals might have played for the NBA title.

Cincinnati fans' hopes were bolstered the next season by the addition of 6-foot-8 center Jerry Lucas, a three-time college All-American at Ohio State. Lucas became the team's "Mr. Inside," while Robertson was "Mr. Outside." Between them, the two players averaged more than 50 points a game during Lucas' rookie year, as the Royals finished the regular season just two games behind the Celtics. Cincinnati was now a great offensive squad—the best in the league—but it just didn't have the defensive strength or depth to handle

Wayman Tisdale, Mr. Inside of today's Kings.

During the season, Oscar Robertson recorded his 15,000th point, 5,000th assist, and 5,000th rebound.

the Celtics in the playoffs. Boston quickly eliminated the Royals on its way to a sixth consecutive NBA championship.

The Royals remained a contender throughout the mid-1960s, the team's most competitive era. Yet local fans wondered if the club would ever defeat the hated Celtics. In an attempt to capture some of the Celtics' magic for themselves, the Royals hired former Boston great Bob Cousy as head coach in 1969. Cousy wanted to develop the same fast-break offense in Cincinnati that he had used in Boston, a style of play that wasn't suited to the skills of Robertson and Lucas. Soon, both Royals heroes were gone in trades. Within a few years, each would win a championship ring—Robertson with the Milwaukee Bucks in 1971, and Lucas with the New York Knicks in 1973. Each would also find his way to the Hall of Fame.

ARCHIBALD AND LACEY AND THE MOVE TO KC

In order to develop his "Celtic-style" offense, coach Cousy needed a strong rebounder and a talented floor general. He found both in the 1970 college draft. The Royals' first two selections that year were 6-foot-10 center "Slammin' Sam" Lacey and 5-foot-11 guard Nate Archibald, fittingly nicknamed "Tiny." They would be the team's leaders throughout the early 1970s.

Newcomer Sam Lacey scored over 1,000 points while leading the team in rebounds.

Lacey started the 1970-71 season slowly and was almost cut from the team. But he found himself by midseason, and soon became one of the top centers in the league. During one game against All-Star Willis Reed of the Knicks, Lacey scored 27 points, grabbed 25 rebounds, and blocked five of Reed's shots. "That was the most complete game I've seen a center in our league play in some time," gushed Cousy.

Archibald also had a fine rookie season. "The little lefty may be the best second-round choice in years," declared basketball writer Jim O'Brien. "He's small and skinny, but he surprised a lot of people with his nonstop play."

Archibald's energy and basketball skills had been surprising people for a long time—even when he was a kid growing up in New York City's rugged South Bronx area. "I wanted to play basketball all the time then," he recalled. "I'd find out there was going to be a game and I'd be there waiting. The older guys would always say, 'Well, we'll let him play. He's small; he'll get tired and quit.' But I never would."

Cousy appreciated Archibald's tirelessness, and, during the guard's second season, "Tiny" was given almost complete control of the club's offense. He responded by leading the Royals in both scoring and assists and being selected second-team All-NBA. The next season he was even more

The Kings are known for tough defense (pages 18-19).

During his dream season, Nate Archibald led the NBA in minutes played, averaging 46 per game.

spectacular, averaging 34 points and 11.4 assists per game. He became the first man in NBA history to lead the league in those two categories in the same year.

Archibald played his dream season before a new set of hometown fans—two sets, in fact. Prior to the 1972-73 season, the Royals changed their name to the Kings and began playing their home games in Kansas City, Missouri, and Omaha, Nebraska. (In 1975, the club settled in Kansas City alone.) Unfortunately, neither the move nor the fine play of Archibald, Lacey, and guard Nate Williams could turn the Kings into a winning team. The club finished with a 36-46 record and failed to make the playoffs for the sixth straight year.

When KC-Omaha got off to a slow start the next year, Cousy was fired and replaced by assistant coach Phil Johnson. Under Johnson, the team made a solid turnaround, going 27-30 over the last two-thirds of the season. Then, in 1974-75, the Kings compiled the franchise's best record in a decade, 44-38, and made the playoffs for the first time since 1967. Joining the club that year was a rookie forward named Scott Wedman, whose deadly accurate outside jumper would become a standard feature of Kings play for many years.

When the club faltered again in 1975-76, coach Johnson made an important, yet controversial, decision. He traded Tiny Archibald to the New Jersey Nets for two first-round draft picks. Although there were cries of outrage from the Kansas City fans, these cries were quieted when the draft choices resulted in the selection of guards Otis Birdsong in 1977 and Phil Ford in 1978.

1 9 7 9

Guard Phil Ford's all-around play earned him the NBA's Rookie of the Year award.

FITZSIMMONS BUILDS A CONTENDER

Birdsong and Ford brought a bright new spirit to the team. "They're like two peas in a pod," said new head coach Cotton Fitzsimmons, who took over for Johnson in 1978-79. "They're a couple of professional comedians who just happen to play ball in the NBA. They're the guys who keep this team loose, and you have to be loose to play basketball."

Fitzsimmons' Kings were not only loose, they were talented. With Birdsong, Ford, Wedman, Lacey, and forward Bill Robinzine leading the way, the club blazed to a 48-34 record in 1978-79 and its first division title in 27 years.

The club had another winning season in 1979-80, and then staged a near-miracle in 1980-81. Although the Kings put together only a 40-42 record that year, they did manage to slip into the playoffs. And coach Fitzsimmons thought they might be able to defy the odds and do well in the post-

Guard Otis Birdsong.

season. "In terms of individual talent, I think you would have to say there is not a lot here," the coach commented. "But our club has chemistry. Nobody's going to beat us badly in the playoffs. We've got too much character."

Kansas City's chances seemed even slimmer when both Phil Ford and Otis Birdsong were lost to injuries. Yet with Ernie Grunfeld and Scott Wedman in the backcourt, the Kings got by both Portland and Phoenix to reach the Western Conference finals. Then Kansas City's Cinderella season came to an abrupt halt when Houston quickly eliminated the Kings in five games. Nevertheless, the seven playoff victories were the most in franchise history.

The Kings' front office still wasn't satisfied with the club's performance, however. Before the next season began, Birdsong, Wedman, and Lacey departed in a series of trades that destroyed the team's chemistry. Despite the arrival of talented young players—such as Mike Woodson, Reggie Theus, Larry Drew, Otis Thorpe, and Eddie Johnson—the club would reach the playoffs only once more during its stay in Kansas City.

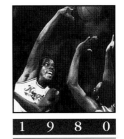

1 9 8 0

Sam Lacey led the Kings in rebounding for the ninth time in 10 years.

SEARCHING FOR GOLD IN SACRAMENTO

While the Kings were in their down period in the early 1980s, a group of six businessmen in Sacramento negotiated to purchase the club at a cost of $10.5 million. Their idea was to relocate the team in the California capital as soon as possible. The new owners believed that Sacramento's growing population could support an NBA team, and that solid rivalries could be built between a Sacramento club and those already in Oakland, Los Angeles, and Portland. The move required the approval of the rest of the NBA own-

Left to right: Eddie Johnson, LaSalle Thompson, Otis Thorpe, Reggie Theus.

ers, however, and getting this took several years. Finally, in April 1985, the relocation was formally approved. Like the gold rushers in 1849, the Kings headed for Sacramento.

"Sacramento is a growing, thriving, world-class city," asserted a beaming Joe Benvenuti, part-owner of the Kings. "We're confident the entire community will welcome the Kings with open arms and support our ultimate goal, to bring a championship to Sacramento."

Benvenuti's smile became even brighter as he noted the huge crowds that greeted the Kings at each home game in their first year in California. Playing in a temporary arena that seated only 10,333, the Kings performed before packed houses all season.

The players responded to their new fans with renewed enthusiasm. Reggie Theus averaged more than 18 points per game and ranked third in the league in assists, and center LaSalle Thompson was eighth in the NBA in rebounding. Team leader Eddie Johnson not only adjusted to becoming the club's sixth man, he thrived in the role, averaging a club-leading 18.7 points per game. Directed by coach Phil Johnson, back for a second stint at the team's helm, the Kings won 25 of their 41 home games and reached the playoffs in their first year in Sacramento.

Unfortunately, the emotion and energy that had carried the Kings through their first season in California quickly disappeared. The club got off to a terrible start in 1986-87, and, partway through the season, Johnson was replaced by assistant coach Jerry Reynolds. But Reynolds had no magic formula for success, either. While the Kings—particularly Theus, Johnson, and Otis Thorpe—did put a lot of points on the board, their porous defense allowed opponents to score even more.

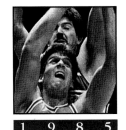

1 9 8 5

Arkansas center Joe Kleine became the first draft choice ever made by the Sacramento Kings.

Forward Otis Thorpe (pages 26-27).

Over the next few years, the Kings made moves—lots of moves. Coaches were brought in. Coaches were sent out. Players were brought in. Players were traded away. It was as if Sacramento's Arco Arena had a revolving door.

First, to improve the defense, the legendary Bill Russell—often called the greatest defensive player of all time—was brought in as head coach and then general manager in 1987-88. The move turned out to be a disaster, and Russell was gone after two seasons. During the Russell era, the Kings drafted such players as Kenny Smith, Pervis Ellison, and Ricky Berry, and traded for such others as Wayman Tisdale, Danny Ainge, and Rodney McCray. Only Tisdale has had a successful career in Sacramento, and was still on the team in 1991.

Danny Ainge's 45 points vs. Golden State is still a Sacramento Kings scoring record.

MOTTA TRIES TO ESTABLISH A WINNING ATTITUDE

Amidst all of the changes, the Kings also brought in a new coach—veteran Dick Motta. Motta had previously built powerful teams in Chicago, Washington, and Dallas, and he hoped to do the same in Sacramento. Motta came on board for the last half of the 1989-90 season, and was far from impressed by what he saw. "When I walked off the court at the end of the season, I wasn't very proud," Motta said. "That was mainly because we didn't compete in a manner that was up to NBA standards. There is a defeatist attitude here. I'm tired of it."

Motta was determined to change both the team's attitude and its personnel. In a series of daring moves, the Kings traded away center Pervis Ellison, the first pick overall in the 1989 college draft; club MVP Rodney McCray; and several reserves. In return, the Kings stockpiled a series of first-round

1 9 9 1

Lionel Simmons ran a close second to New Jersey's Derrick Coleman in the Rookie of the Year voting.

draft choices. They used four of those draft picks in 1990 to add Lionel Simmons, Anthony Bonner, Duane Causwell, and Travis Mays to the team.

The real find in the draft turned out to be Simmons. Nick-named "L-Train," the 6-foot-7 small forward chugged his way to club leadership in both scoring and rebounding during his first season and was named to the NBA All-Rookie team. "He's a great rebounder and scorer who can also handle and pass the ball," said Kings general manager Jerry Reynolds. "We're confident he'll be a solid player in our league for a long, long time."

Despite Simmons' achievements, the Kings finished the 1990-91 season in the Pacific Division cellar, mainly because of an abysmal 1-40 record on the road. So the club began wheeling and dealing again. First, Travis Mays was sent to Atlanta for sparkplug guard Spud Webb. Then, when the

First-round draft pick Anthony Bonner.

Offensive spark plug Spud Webb.

1 9 9 2

In his first season with the Kings, Mitch Richmond led the club in scoring and three-point shooting.

Kings were unable to sign top draft pick Billy Owens, they traded his draft rights to Golden State for superstar guard Mitch Richmond. Richmond quickly became the team's all-around leader.

Motta announced before the 1991-92 season that he was confident the club's lineup of Causwell in the middle, Tisdale and Simmons at forward, and Richmond and Webb at guard could be successful. "We've improved our team both depth-wise and from the standpoint of athletic ability. Now it's a matter of how we blend together. I like the direction we're going in," the coach said.

Motta's confidence and his relationship with the Kings players eroded quickly when the team got off to another bad start. At midseason, Motta was fired and replaced on an interim basis by assistant coach Rex Hughes. It will be up to Hughes or his replacement to bring stability to the team and to rebuild fan interest in the club.

Club captain Wayman Tisdale summed it up best when he said, "I've been frustrated here because I really want to win. When you don't win, there is no glory." The Sacramento Kings are still searching for gold in the NBA. Their fans are hoping they'll "strike it rich" soon.